# THE CORSICAN BROTHERS

# Borgo Press Books by ALEXANDRE DUMAS

*Anthony*
*The Barricade at Clichy*
*Bathilda*
*Caligula*
*The Corsican Brothers* (with Eugène Grangé & Xavier de Montépin)
*The Count of Monte Cristo, Part One: The Betrayal of Edmond Dantès*
*The Count of Monte Cristo, Part Two: The Resurrection of Edmond Dantès*
*The Count of Monte Cristo, Part Three: The Rise of Monte Cristo*
*The Count of Monte Cristo, Part Four: The Revenge of Monte Cristo*
*A Fairy Tale* (with Adolphe de Leuven and Léon Lhérie)
*The Gold Thieves*
*Kean*
*The Last of the Three Musketeers; or, The Prisoner of the Bastille* (Musketeers #3)
*Lorenzino*
*The Mohican's War*
*Napoléon Bonaparte*
*Queen Margot*
*Richard Darlington* (with Prosper Dinaux)
*Sylvandire*
*The Three Musketeers* (Musketeers #1)
*The Three Musketeers—Twenty Years Later* (Musketeers #2)
*The Tower of Nesle* (with Frédéric Gaillardet)
*The Two Dianas* (with Paul Meurice)
*Urbain Grandier and the Devils of Loudon*
*The Venetian*
*The Whites and the Blues*
*The Widow's Husband; and, Porthos in Search of an Outfit*
*Young Louix XIV*

RELATED DRAMAS:

*The Queen's Necklace*, by Pierre Decourcelle
*The Seed of the Musketeers*, by Paul de Kock & Guénée (Musketeers #5)
*The San Felice*, by Maurice Drack
*The Son of Porthos the Musketeer*, by Émile Blavet (Musketeers #4)
*A Summer Night's Dream*, Adolphe de Leuven & Joseph-Bernard Rosier
*The Widow's Husband; and, Porthos in Search of an Outfit: Two Dumasian Comedies*, edited by Frank J. Morlock

# THE CORSICAN BROTHERS

A PLAY IN THREE ACTS

ALEXANDRE DUMAS

With Eugène Grangé & Xavier de Montépin

Adapted and Translated by Frank J. Morlock

THE BORGO PRESS
MMXII

THE CORSICAN BROTHERS
Copyright © 2004, 2012 by Frank J. Morlock

FIRST BORGO PRESS EDITION

Published by Wildside Press LLC

www.wildsidebooks.com

# DEDICATION

For my grandsons,
Miles, Nicholas, and Sebastian

# CONTENTS

CAST OF CHARACTERS . . . . . . . . . . . . . .9
ACT I, Scene 1 . . . . . . . . . . . . . . . . . 11
ACT II, Scene 2. . . . . . . . . . . . . . . . . 75
ACT II, Scene 3. . . . . . . . . . . . . . . . 107
ACT II, Scene 4. . . . . . . . . . . . . . . . 139
ACT III, Scene 5 . . . . . . . . . . . . . . . 143
ABOUT THE AUTHOR . . . . . . . . . . . . . 175

## CAST OF CHARACTERS

### THE CORSICAN BROTHERS

Fabien dei Franchi (Fechter)

Louis dei Franche

Fabien dei Franche Berthallet

Château-Renaud

Alfred Meyard

Gordane Martilli

Montgeron

Colonna

Orlando

LeBuchaon

The Justice of the Peace

The Guide

A Servant

Griffo

A Surgeon

Mme Savilia dei Franchi

Emilie de Lespare

Esther

Grain d'or

Pomponette

Maria

A dominer

Corsican peasants, young people, Domonis, Monks, etc.

# ACT I
## SCENE 1

*In Corsica in the village of Sullarno, Province of Sarture, at the home of Mme Savilia dei Franchi.*

*The principal room of the house—large chimney surmounted by a trophy of carbines hung from the horns of a wild ram.*

*At the back—an entry door. On both sides, doors.*

*AT RISE, Maria is seated to the left, singing and sewing.*

MARIA

From Alry to Sartene, the way is very fine. But hardly have you left the place then you find a tomb.

A stand of rose laurel.
Is its only decoration
A stream of water irrigates it
And that's where
My love Peppino—reposes.

(knocking at the door)

(rising)

It seems to me someone is knocking.

(more knocking)

Why, yes, I'm not mistaken.

(calling)

Griffo! Griffo!

(Griffo entering from the right.)

GRIFFO

Well? What's wrong? Is there a fire in the house?

MARIA

No, but a rapping at the door.

GRIFFO

Go open!

MARIA

(fearfully)

It's too late, thanks.

GRIFFO

Coward.

(goes to open and disappears)

MARIA

(alone and fixing her spinning wheel)

Good! Go open to receive some pistol shot or some knife blow.

(Griffo returns).

MARIA

Well, who was there?

GRIFFO

A French traveler who's just arrived from Sullacaro, and who requests hospitality.

MARIA

(with joy)

A French traveler! You didn't refuse him, I hope.

GRIFFO

Refuse! Right, are things like that refused in Corsica?

On the contrary, I answered that Madame Savilia dei Franchi, our mistress, would be honored to receive him.

MARIA

And this traveler?

GRIFFO

Well, he's dismounting his horse! You, run to announce his visit.

MARIA

To whom?

GRIFFO

Why, to the Countess, it seems to me, come on, get going, you will see him later, then as he's sleeping, here, you will have plenty of time.

MARIA

Ah, ah—indeed!

(she leaves by the left)

GRIFFO

(in the back)

This way, Excellence, this way. They've gone to inform Signora Savilia to receive you. Meanwhile, please rest.

ALFRED

Truly, my friend, I fear upsetting her—to be indiscreet.

GRIFFO

(smiling)

Indiscreet! Ah, sir, that's a word the French don't understand. In Corsica, a stranger does honor to the house that he stops at.

(turning)

Hello, Tomaso—place the baggage of His Excellency—don't worry about a thing, sir, all this will be transported to your room.

GUIDE

You see, Excellency, that I was right to tell you you have not been badly inspired in choosing for your hostel, the house of Signora Savilia.

ALFRED

No, certainly. And I see that I can dismiss you now, here, two piastres—one for the mule, one for the master. Are you satisfied?

GRIFFO

I should say so; you pay me like my animal!

ALFRED

(to Griffo)

As to the rest, it wasn't just chance that led me to the house of your mistress, my friend.

GRIFFO

Does Your Excellency know the Signora Savilia?

ALFRED

No, I don't have that honor but I am carrying a letter of recommendation to her.

GRIFFO

Oh! You have no need of that to be welcome.

ALFRED

Still, my friend, permit me to believe that in presenting myself on behalf of her son.

GRIFFO

(excitedly)

Mr. Louis?

ALFRED

Exactly.

SAVILIA

(entering from the left)

You are coming on behalf of my son, you say, sir?

ALFRED

(bowing slightly)

Madame, you must think me very bold, but the custom of the country excuses me, and this letter—

(giving it to her)

—from Louis authorizes me.

SAVILIA

(taking the letter)

Oh, you have no need of this recommendation, sir, to be greeted in this house as you deserve to be. In Corsica, all travelers can, on entering a town or a village, toss the bridle on the neck of horse and dismount wherever it stops. Every door will open before him, without need of knocking. Once entered into the house, he'll dwell there as long as he pleases—and at his departure, those who received him will thank him for the honor. He really wanted to do them.

(turning)

Maria—you will prepare for this gentleman the room Louis occupied before his departure. Griffo, take the bags of our guest—go, so long as the gentleman stays here, you will be in his service.

(The two servants bow.)

BOTH

Yes, Signora.

(They leave carrying the luggage.)

ALFRED

My stay will not be long, Madame, and I will not abuse the hospitality you've had the kindness to offer me. My voyage is coming near its end. Important business is calling me to Paris—and tomorrow, Madame, I will regretfully take my leave of you.

SAVILIA

You are free to do what suits you, sir, yet I hope you will change your mind and we will have the honor of possessing you longer.

ALFRED

(bowing slightly)

Madame—

SAVILIA

In any case, you've heard what I said to my servants: The house is like them, sir—it belongs to you completely—use it then as if it were yours and will be welcome to the mother as you were going to be to the son as soon as he returns.

ALFRED

Ah! That's true, Madame, Mr. Fabien, your second son.

SAVILIA

I have two children, sir, but neither first nor second son. Between them is neither first nor second—they are two brothers, that's all.

ALFRED

Indeed, Louis spoke to me of it, Madame, your two sons are twins, I believe.

SAVILIA

Yes, sir, born the same day, the same instant.

ALFRED

And they resemble each other greatly, I am also told.

SAVILIA

You will judge for yourself when you see Fabien.

ALFRED

And will I soon have that pleasure?

SAVILIA

Oh, in all probability. He left Sullacaro this morning, early to get to the mountain where he had a meeting, he cannot delay returning.

ALFRED

I've hastened to see him, to shake his hand on behalf of his brother, but I beg your mercy, Madame, that I am not depriving you of reading this letter.

SAVILIA

Thanks. You understand that happiness that a mother always has in seeing the writing of a son from whom she is separated.

(she sits to the left and quietly reads)

My dear Louis—he commands you to me as one of his friends, you will do me the justice of telling him that I didn't wait for his recommendation.

ALFRED

Oh! Madame, you've been a hundred times too good! He will know it and that won't surprise him. For the rest, if he doesn't keep you engaged in that letter longer, he wanted to give me the pleasure of myself giving you his news.

SAVILIA

Is the news good?

ALFRED

Excellent, Madame, Louis was marvelously well when I left him and—

GRIFFO

(entering by the back and coming forward)

Madame, it's Mr. Fabien.

SAVILIA

(rising)

Fabien! You see, sir, I told you he wouldn't delay.

(to Griffo)

Where is he?

GRIFFO

(pointing to the back)

There, two steps away, he's chatting with our Justice of the Peace.

(to Alfred)

Your Excellency's room is ready and if it pleases you—

ALFRED

Thanks, I am not tired; it's nice to be well received.

(he walks to the upstage right chatting with Griffo to whom he gives his hat and cane)

(Fabien enters carrying a rifle which he puts down on entering.)

SAVILIA

(going to greet him)

Come, come on, Fabien, you are expected here.

FABIEN

By you, Mother?

SAVILIA

Yes, by me, and someone else, too! How slow you are returning, dear.

FABIEN

(low)

Oh! It's that demon of an Orlando who's a true Corsican and was hanging back.

SAVILIA

But, still—

FABIEN

(with a sigh)

In the end, mother, everything is straightened out, agreed—Orlando and Colonna have promised that the two of them will be here this evening with their kinsmen and friends—and since they promised, they will come. But mother, you said someone was waiting for me.

SAVILIA

Mr. Alfred de Meynard, a friend of your brother.

FABIEN

Indeed, mother, I met Tomaso who apprised me that we had a guest, and I was hurrying to come to wish him welcome.

(going to Alfred and offering his hand)

Sir—

ALFRED

(looking at him with astonishment)

Ah! My God!

FABIEN

What's wrong with you?

ALFRED

Oh! What an uncommon resemblance.

FABIEN

(smiling)

Ah, yes, I understand.

ALFRED

Truly, I am tempted to ask you if it is to Mr. Fabien or Mr. Louis dei Franchi that I have the honor to speak to at this moment.

SAVILIA

(who has sat back down)

The gentleman brings us a letter.

FABIEN

(excitedly)

A letter, mother! Will you give it to me?

(opening it)

Ah! It's been three weeks since you left Louis? Then you can't know.

SAVILIA

What's wrong, Fabien?

FABIEN

Oh, nothing mother! I only said that the gentleman left Paris too long ago to bring us important news from my brother.

ALFRED

Pardon me, sir, for not delivering this letter to you sooner, but having only a month for my trip to Corsica, it was impossible for me to deviate from the itinerary of my guide, Valery—so first off, I visited Bastia, Corte, Ajaccio—At last, here I am in the province of Sartene, at Sullacaro, having kept, as you see, the best visit for the last.

FABIEN

Will you allow me, sir, to ask you how my brother was, when you let him?

ALFRED

Why, if you want me to speak of his health, sir, it seemed excellent to me.

FABIEN

So much for the physical side, but as to the moral side, he didn't seem to you to be sad, tortured, uneasy?

ALFRED

Why no, I left him ardently working on his thesis that he's going to pass.

FABIEN

Ah! Yes!

ALFRED

He seemed full of hope and sure of success.

FABIEN

So, at this period, you don't know him to have any cause for pain?

ALFRED

None—would you have some reasons to believe otherwise?

SAVILIA

(uneasily)

My son?

ALFRED

Have you received some bad news since?

FABIEN

Received, no, at least in the sense you give that word.

ALFRED

I don't understand, sir.

FABIEN

I mean that we haven't received a letter from Louis.

ALFRED

You know the French proverb. No news is good news. I don't see anything that should concern you.

FABIEN

Yes, you don't see it, but as for me—?

SAVILIA

I hope, Fabien, that nothing serious has happened to your brother.

FABIEN

(going to her)

Serious? No, mother—I don't think that, yet—

SAVILIA

Yes, this uneasiness of which you spoke to me yesterday. These troubles that you suppose Louis has—

FABIEN

Well, mother, I am still in the same apprehensions.

SAVILIA

Yes, since yesterday you haven't had any other warnings?

FABIEN

(after a moment)

No.

SAVILIA

Still, if some grave danger threatened the life of your brother—?

FABIEN

(with emotion)

Mother!

SAVILIA

If your brother was dead—you would know it, wouldn't you?

FABIEN

Yes, because I would have seen it.

ALFRED

(aside, astonished)

He would have seen it?

SAVILIA

And you would have told me?

FABIEN

(kissing her face)

Yes, mother, I would have told you.

SAVILIA

(rising)

Thanks! The absent are in the hands of the Lord. The main thing is that I am sure your brother is alive. Let's not think of anything else but receiving the guest that good fortune has sent us.

(She curtsies to Alfred, who bows to her. Fabien accompanies his mother to the door on the left. Savilia leaves.)

ALFRED

(to himself, watching them)

Now this is strange! Who is this brother who presents that if his brother was dead he would have seen him again? What kind of mother is this who makes one of her sons promise that if the other is dead, he will tell her?

(gaily)

As to the rest, I am in the land of adventures, and this house seems to me a veritable nest of legends.

FABIEN

(coming close to him)

Sir, you will excuse us for having spoken in this way about our family affairs in front of you? Besides you are not a stranger since you were sent to us by our poor Louis.

(uttering a sigh)

ALFRED

Excuse me, sir, but—

FABIEN

Yes, you are trying to understand, I see that—! The last words exchanged between my mother and me, seem puzzling to you?

ALFRED

I admit it! You said you were without recent news of your brother?

FABIEN

That's true, sir.

FABIEN

True again!

ALFRED

Then, since you are without news of him—what can make you suppose that he may be uneasy, ill, tormented?

FABIEN

Because, for the last three days, I have been uneasy, ill,

tormented!

ALFRED

(smiling)

Pardon, but that explains nothing to me.

FABIEN

You know that Louis and I are twins?

ALFRED

Sir, Louis told me, and just now your mother did me the honor of telling me so again.

FABIEN

You know when we came into the world we were connected to each other like Siamese twins and for several years excited the curiosity of the Parisians.

ALFRED

No, I was unaware of that.

FABIEN

Still, that is the fact on which all that is fantastic in our situation rests; it required a scalpel to separate us. But the moral adhesion has continued; which means that although separated, although distant even, the same heart, even the same soul. The rest of it is that every physical or moral impression, a bit strong—which one of us experiences, has its counterpart on the other.

ALFRED

(who has taken a seat near the table)

Ah, really!

FABIEN

Thus, during the last few days which have just elapsed, for no reason, I've been sad, uneasy, somber; I have experienced heartfelt anguish. It's evident to me, sir, that my brother is experiencing violent pain.

ALFRED

And what sort of pain do you think this may be?

FABIEN

Do I know? I experience the effect, but I am unaware of the cause.

ALFRED

Some reversal in his career, perhaps?

FABIEN

No, sir, no—it's a pain of the heart.

ALFRED

(smiling)

I confess to you that I thought he was more occupied with his studies than with women.

FABIEN

Women! No, I don't think he's occupied with women. I believe he's in love with a woman—which is quite different.

ALFRED

And this woman?

(rising)

But pardon me—I see I am trying to enter indiscreetly into your brother's secrets.

FABIEN

Oh! My God, no, sir, and what I am going to tell you is quite simple.

About a year ago, the daughter of the Commanding

General of Corsica came to Ajaccio to spend two months with her father. She was an adorable person, young, beautiful, gracious. My brother and I had several opportunities to see her, and all our sensations are double, but alike, as we hate and as we love with the same heart, we both became amorous at the same time. Only as each of us perceived the other loving, each of us tried to choke off his love. I don't know if I succeeded for my part, but I believe that I was succeeding, and an increase of tenderness on his part proved to me his gratitude—the general left Corsica to return to France; his daughter followed him and the adorable vision disappeared. Sometime after this departure, my brother asked me if I didn't want to go to Paris to study law or pursue a course in medicine, it had always been agreed between us that we would never leave Corsica at the same time, and that one of us would remain, invariably, close to our mother.

I understood the need of this poor loving heart, and I declared that I have no desire to go to France. At this declaration, I saw joy radiate over the face of my brother. In that case, said he, it's I who will go. Go, my Louis, I said to him, go! And he left. As for me, you can see, I remained in Sullacaro, and I will probably never leave it.

ALFRED

You will never leave this village?

FABIEN

That seems strange to you, doesn't it, that one clings to a wretched country like Corsica? But what do you expect? As for me, I am a sort of product of the island, like green okra, like rose-laurel; I need my atmosphere impregnated with the deep rooted emanations from the mountain and the acres perfumed by the sea. I have to have torrents to cross, my rocks to scale, my forests to explore; I need my rifle, space, independence, freedom—if I was transported into a city it seems to me I would suffocate there as in a prison; I am one of those plants that can only live under an open sky. Everything then is for the best, as you see, my brother will be a lawyer, and as for me—

ALFRED

And as for you?

FABIEN

Oh, as for me, I will be a Corsican.

ALFRED

(laughing)

Oh! Oh! Now there's a characteristic response! And you think that is on account of this woman that your brother has experienced this pain whose echo you felt?

FABIEN

Yes! Although in his letters he's never spoken to me of it, yes, it's because of her!

(placing his hand on his heart)

He is still in love—or rather, more in love than ever; the wound was deep, go!

ALFRED

(gaily)

Luckily, that sort of wound, sir, however deep they may be, rarely become mortal, and, in my opinion, if you have no other cause for worry.

FABIEN

Something has happened to my brother, sir!

ALFRED

Something serious?

FABIEN

Serious, yes, I'm afraid of that!

ALFRED

But still, you don't think he may be in danger?

FABIEN

Oh!

ALFRED

That he may be dead?

FABIEN

Dead! No, for as I told my mother, I would have seen him again.

ALFRED

(astonished)

You would have seen him again. Allow me to tell you that again—there's something in these words—

FABIEN

Incomprehensible to you, and for which you would really like to ask an explanation from me, right?

ALFRED

I admit it! If this explanation may at all times enter a

profane ear—

FABIEN

No question, but—

ALFRED

Pardon, sir, I am going from one indiscretion to another!

FABIEN

No, only you are a man of the world and consequently your mind is a bit skeptical—I fear there to see you treat as a fable a fact which belongs, it's true, much more to legend than to history, but which, such as it is, exists in the family for the last 300 years.

ALFRED

Oh! If it's only that fear that is stopping you, let me reassure you—no one in matters of traditions and legends is more credulous than I am—if there are things in this world that I must be particular about, it's unbelievable things.

FABIEN

In that case, you might believe in apparitions?

ALFRED

Why not?

FABIEN

Oh, in that case, listen to me for you are my man. (sitting by the table) Well, here's the fact that's been kept in the home of the Franchis like a family tradition—300 years ago our great, great grandfather Bartholomew dei Franchi died leaving two sons orphaned of father and mother. These two children isolated in the world understood their isolation and loved each other with all the love they had for their father and mother, if their father and mother had lived. This love became proverbial in the country, and as if to give it a sanction more holy still than the natural sentiment which united them,—to give it the sanction of an oath they swore to each other that nothing would separate them, not even death, and as a result of knowing only the powerful configuration, they each wrote with their blood on a parchment that they exchanged, that solemn promise, that reciprocal engagement, that the first to die would appear to the other—at the very moment of his death and even in all the supreme moments of his life.

ALFRED

Well?

# FABIEN

Three months after this magical ceremony took place, one of these two brothers who was in a vendetta with a powerful Corsican family fell in an ambush and was killed at the very moment when his brother, uneasy about him, was sealing a letter he had just written to him, but as he pressed the seal of his ring into the still fuming wax, he heard a sigh behind him, and turning, he saw his brother, standing, hand placed on his shoulder although he didn't feel the hand.

Then by a mechanical movement, he offered the letter which was destined for him; the other took it sadly, shook his head, and pointing with his hand towards the window of the room, he commanded the wall to open. The wall obeyed, and then the survivor was present at the scene of the murder; he saw his brother struggle and fall into the hands of the murderers in a way that he found himself face to face with these men; whom he had never seen, not only did he recognize them, but he was to go find even the least detail of their crime, even to the depth of the obscurity within which the assassins thought to enshroud themselves.

Well, my dear guest, the two brothers, from what it seemed, had engaged not only for themselves, but for their descendants, because after this time, the apparitions continued in the family, at the moment of death of those who passed away as well as the signs of all events that must occur.

ALFRED

But as for you, you haven't had any apparition—?

FABIEN

No, not yet.

ALFRED

Then you can be sure that Louis is still alive.

FABIEN

It's true Louis is still alive, but I fear he may be injured.

ALFRED

(rising)

Injured? How, by whom?

FABIEN

Imagine that it is morning as I was going up the mountain—

(Savilia appears)

Silence! Here's my mother; not a word in front of her, I beg you.

ALFRED

Oh, don't worry.

(Griffo and Maria bring in supper, which they place on the table at the right.)

SAVILIA

Gentlemen, whenever you like, dinner is waiting.

(to Fabien)

Well?

FABIEN

Well, mother, here I am and perfectly confident. Let's eat, then, you hear, Mr. Meynard.

(they sit at the table, Fabien continues with forced gaiety)

So then, my dear guest, you've decided to come see Corsica? You did will to hasten, because in a few years, thanks to the mania for progress and civilization that's afoot, those who are coming to seek Corsica will no longer find it.

ALFRED

In any case, sir, if the old national spirit of Sampiero

and Paoli recoils before civilization and seeks refuge in some corner of the island, it will quite certainly be in the province of Sareno and the valley of Tavaro where it will find asylum.

SAVILIA

(smiling)

You think so, sir?

ALFRED

But it seems to me, Madame, that I have around me a fine and noble picture of old Corsican customs.

FABIEN

Yes, and yet, sir, between my mother and me, facing 300 years of memories in this same house of crenellations and fortifications, the French spirit came to seek my brother, to carry him away from us and transported him to Paris—from which he will return a lawyer if he returns.

SAVILIA

What are you saying?

FABIEN

Nothing, mother, or rather, indeed I am saying he will

reside in Ajaccio, instead of living in the old house of his fathers; I am saying he will sue over the boundaries, the common walls, the easements! If he has some talent, he will become King's attorney, perhaps—then he will pursue the poor devils who, as they say in the country, you make or unmake a skin; he confounds the assassin with the murderer as is the custom in France; he will ask in the name of the law for the heads of those who will have done what their fathers would have regarded as a dishonor not to do, and in the evening, because of the strength of words, of gestures of his sometimes he will have secured a head for the executioner; he will think he's served the country, have brought his stone to the temple of civilization, as our prefect said. Ah! My God! My God!

ALFRED

But, sir, you clearly see that God wanted to counterbalance things since by making your brother a votary of new principles, he's made you a partisan of old customs. Mathematically, it seems to me, two equal forces will neutralize each other.

FABIEN

Me, sir? Even in this moment I am not like others paying my tribute to the Metropolis? Am I not in the process of accomplishing an action that my ancestors would have regarded as unworthy of them?

ALFRED

You, sir?

FABIEN

Well, my God, yes, me! Perhaps you have heard that our peasants are divided into two factions.

ALFRED

Yes—that of the Orlandi and the Colonna; they promised me at the Ajaccio I don't know how many murders, assassinations, traps and ambushes—and I admit to you I was counting on you a little to—

FABIEN

Well! No sooner said than done! You counted without your host—Do you know what I am doing admits rifle shots, knife blows, dagger thrusts? I am arbitrating.

ALFRED

Arbitrating?

FABIEN

You came to us to see a vendetta! Well, you are going to see something even more rare; you are going to see a reconciliation.

ALFRED

A reconciliation.

FABIEN

Which will be no easy thing, I'll answer for that, seeing the degree to which things have come to—

ALFRED

And on what account came this great quarrel, that, thanks to you, is on the point of being extinguished?

FABIEN

Truly, I don't know very well how to tell you about it—the first cause.

ALFRED

Well?

FABIEN

The first cause was a chicken.

ALFRED

(astonished)

A chicken?

FABIEN

Yes, you see about ten years ago, a chicken escaped from the courtyard of the Orlandi and sought refuge in that of the Colonna; the Orlandi demanded the chicken; the Colonna maintained that it was theirs; in the midst of the discussion an Orlando had the evil inspiration to threaten the Colonna and to denounce them to a justice of the peace and to denounce them under oath.

To this threat, an old Colonna, the ancestor of the whole family, who held the chicken in his hand, wrung its neck and threw it in the face of the Mother of the Orlandi. Heavens, said she, since it's your chicken, eat it.

On this, an Orlando picked up the chicken by its feet, and raising his hand and the chicken, so as to strike the one who had thrown it in the face of his sister; but at that moment he raised his hand, a Colonna, who had by his rifle loaded, fired at close range into his chest, killing him.

ALFRED

Truly! And how many lives have paid for this ridiculous squabble?

FABIEN

There've been nine dead and five wounded.

ALFRED

And that for a wretched chicken!

FABIEN

Yes.

ALFRED

And without doubt, it's at the behest of these families that you are mediating to put an end to this quarrel?

FABIEN

Oh—not at all! They would be exterminated to the last man before taking a step towards the other! No, no, it's the request of my brother who has spoken to the keeper of the seals; I ask you a bit, why they are meddling in Paris—? It's the prefect who has played us this trick, pretending that if I wanted to say a word all this would end like a vaudeville—with a marriage and a couple of lines of poetry to the public.

So, he addressed himself to my brother, who took the ball on the rebound and wrote me that he had given his word for me—what do you expect? I couldn't let it be said down there that a dei Franchi would have engaged the word of his brother and that his brother had not honored the engagement. With the result that, this is the evening that the ceremony of reconciliation is to take place—here this every evening.

(clocks outside are heard)

Wait, do you hear?

Here are the parish clocks which are conveying the solemnity to the whole world.

GRIFFO

(entering by the door at the left)

Mr. Fabien.

FABIEN

What?

GRIFFO

(low)

There's someone who wishes to speak to you.

FABIEN

Who is it?

GRIFFO

(low)

Orlando.

FABIEN

Well—how marvelous; show him in—

(going to the door at the left)

Hey, come in my dear Orlando.

ORLANDO

(entering, tugged by Fabien)

Pardon, but in truth.

FABIEN

What?

ORLANDO

In truth—why it's that—

FABIEN

Will you come in!

ORLANDO

I'm coming in, I'm coming in—that's very easy for you to say—but I'd rather not come in—

FABIEN

Well?

ORLANDO

Mr. Fabien, it's for me to say, you see that it's really hard to reconcile with an enemy.

FABIEN

Orlando, I thought I had your word—

ORLANDO

Certainly you've got it! Oh! If you didn't have it—

FABIEN

Look, Orlando, isn't all the advantage to you? Recapitulate. Haven't five Colonna been killed versus four Orlandi?

ORLANDO

I know quite well it's a consideration—but it doesn't matter.

MARIA

(entering from the right with dessert)

Mr. Fabien?

FABIEN

What do you want?

MARIA

There's someone who's asking for you.

FABIEN

Where?

MARIA

(pointing to the right)

FABIEN

Do you know who it is?

MARIA

I think it's a Colonna.

FABIEN

Fine! Make him come in.

(to Griffo)

You, turn that way, and go lock the door from the

outside.

GRIFFO

(leaving by the left)

Ah, yes, I understand.

FABIEN

(who has kept Orlando by the sleeve throughout his asides with Maria and Griffo)

I tell you, Orlando, that you have the best position.

ORLANDO

But it comes with its chicken, at least.

FABIEN

It comes with its chicken.

ORLANDO

A white chicken?

FABIEN

Oh! Black or white—

ORLANDO

White! White!

FABIEN

White!

ORLANDO

And alive!

FABIEN

Alive!

ORLANDO

First of all, nothing doing if it's dead.

FABIEN

It will be alive.

ORLANDO

And he will offer his hand first.

FABIEN

Oh—both together it's agreed.

ORLANDO

I still was thinking—

FABIEN

(forcefully)

Both together! Yeah! An Orlando will fade in memory when it's a question of recollecting his word?

ORLANDO

(with a great sigh)

Ah! Still it's tough! Happily there are five Colonna dead as against four Orlando.

FABIEN

(to Colonna who enters pushed by Maria)

Get in here, you!

COLONNA

Is it absolutely necessary?

(Meanwhile, Orlando has approached the door and attempted to leave; but having found it is locked from outside, he has resumed his place and looks at Colonna with ferocious eyes.)

FABIEN

By Jove! It is necessary!

COLONNA

You see, it's because there had been one Colonna the more killed at our place.

FABIEN

Well, yes, I know that, but there were four more Orlandi wounded as against one Colonna.

COLONNA

Oh, you know quite well it doesn't count except one is dead.

FABIEN

Good—it's no longer a question of all that. Have you got the chicken?

COLONNA

The chicken?

FABIEN

Wasn't it agreed that you would come with a chicken?

COLONNA

Yes, it was agreed.

FABIEN

Where is it?

COLONNA

It's here.

FABIEN

Here, where?

COLONNA

In my pocket.

FABIEN

And white?

COLONNA

Oh! White—with a little black spot.

FABIEN

(low)

I will take responsibility for the spot—but alive?

COLONNA

That is to say I brought it living, but cannot answer, that en route it may be dead—I was a bit seated over it and—

FABIEN

Let's see it!

(to Griffo)

Go lock the door from outside.

(Colonna delivers the chicken to Fabien)

The Devil. Just in time—hold this chicken and wait—

COLONNA

(to Fabien)

At least, since I'm bringing the chicken, he will offer his hand first?

FABIEN

Both at once, it's agreed.

COLONNA

Was it agreed?

COLONNA

Come on, Colonna!

COLONNA

(with a sigh)

Ah! Damn! If it's agreed, a Colonna has only his word.

FABIEN

(to Orlando

Who is your sponsor?

ORLANDO

Andrea Mari.

FABIEN

(to Colonna)

And you?

COLONNA

(with an air of amazement)

My sponsor?

**FABIEN**

Yes!

**COLONNA**

Eh! I didn't think to bring one.

**ORLANDO**

(wanting to leave)

If there's no sponsor, deal's off.

**FABIEN**

(grabbing him)

He has a sponsor, Mr. Alfred de Meynard—you will serve as a sponsor for a Colonna?

**ALFRED**

Willingly.

**FABIEN**

Open to everybody.

(Savilia and Alfred have risen. They go to open the door at the back)

(Enter the Justice of the Peace and the relatives and friends of the two adversaries.)

MR. JUSTICE OF THE PEACE

(after having installed himself at the table)

My friends, Mr. Fabien dei Franchi has gathered us in this house, dwelled in by his ancestors of three centuries to be present at one of those events which rejoice the mind of man and the heart of God.

(the two adversaries grumble)

Each of you receive this wild olive branch, symbol of peace, and swear, forgetting the past, friendship in the future.

COLONNA

Forget, so be it, friendship, no!

ORLANDO

You hear!

COLONNA

Damn! It isn't you who are giving the chicken.

FABIEN

(giving him an olive branch)

Friendship in the future, Orlando!

ORLANDO

We'll try.

FABIEN

(giving him an olive branch)

You hear, Colonna? Friendship in the future.

COLONNA

We'll do all we can.

FABIEN

Good, it's agreed—now give each other your hands.

(finding Orlando and leading him to center stage, then going after Colonna. While he gets Colonna, Orlando slips back to his place. He gestures to Alfred who leads Orlando from his side, while he brings Colonna.)

FABIEN

Come, the hands!

MR. JUSTICE OF THE PEACE

(reading)

Before us, Antonio Sarrola, Justice of the Peace of Sullacaro, province of Sartene, between Gaetaur Orlandi, and Marco Colonna; having been solemnly agreed to the following—beginning from this day, the 22nd of March 1841—then the vendetta declared between them since he 11th of February 1830—will cease.

In faith of which they have signed the documents before the principals of the village, with their witnesses, Mr. Fabien dei Franchi, arbitrator, the relatives of each of the two contracting parties, and before us, the justice of the peace.

FABIEN

Come, Colonna, the chicken!

(Colonna makes a movement as if to lash the face of Orlando, but under Fabien's glare, controls himself and politely presents the chicken.)

MR. JUSTICE OF THE PEACE

Now, sign!

ORLANDO

I don't know how to sign.

MR. JUSTICE OF THE PEACE

Make your cross.

(Orlando, after many difficulties decides to make his mark. It's the same for Colonna, to whom Fabien brings the papers to sign. After which the Justice of the Peace invites the witnesses to sign. Meanwhile, Fabien goes to Orlando, who looks at the chicken.)

FABIEN

(to Orlando)

Well, Orlando, here it is all straightened out.

ORLANDO

(low)

Hum! Excellency, the chicken is a bit emaciated,

(Everybody signs—general exit.)

FABIEN

You see, my dear guest, that's how things take place today in Corsica and say that we are not worthy of taking our place in the number of civilized nations.

ALFRED

Well, I am enchanted; at least I will have something very new to tell all my predecessors.

SAVILIA

You will tell the thing to Louis won't you, sir; you will tell him how all of this took place in front of us, and how brother acquitted the word of brother?

ALFRED

Ah, don't worry, I won't fail.

SAVILIA

Now it is late, you must be worn out, sir. Griffo, escort our guest to his room.

FABIEN

Mother, give that duty to Maria, I have some orders to give Griffo.

SAVILIA

Neither Maria nor Griffo will be delegated to escort our guest to the door of his room, it will be me.

ALFRED

Oh, Madame, I won't allow it!

SAVILIA

It was the duty of ancient Chatelaines and in Corsica we are still in the sixteenth century.

ALFRED

(low to Fabien)

Goodnight! Don't forget that I'm not relieving you of ending your story.

FABIEN

Yes, till tomorrow.

ALFRED

Since you insist, Madame.

(leaving to the right with Savilia and Maria)

FABIEN

Griffo?

GRIFFO

Sir?

FABIEN

You've got to get ready to leave.

GRIFFO

For where?

FABIEN

For Ajaccio.

GRIFFO

When's this?

FABIEN

Right away.

GRIFFO

And what am I to do in Ajaccio?

FABIEN

You will stay there until the arrival of a letter from Paris; once this letter has arrived, you will mount your horse and return here hell for leather.

GRIFFO

Ah! My God! Do you then have some uneasiness about

your brother?

FABIEN

Griffo, my brother is wounded; the great thing to know is if it's more or less dangerous.

GRIFFO

You've been warned?

FABIEN

Yes, this morning; listen, I tell you this to double your zeal, my dear Griffo; but not a word to my mother; you understand?

GRIFFO

Not a word; it's agreed.

FABIEN

This morning; here's what I didn't tell our traveler; this morning as I was climbing the mountain, I experienced suddenly a pain in my side, like the blade of a sword running through my breast; I turned. I looked around me. I placed my hand on my breast; no wound, a pain, that's all. Oh! Then you understand, I saw plainly that is was not I who had just been struck. Then my heart knotted up, terror seized me, and I screamed. My brother, some misfortune has happened to my brother!

I looked at my watch—it was 9:10.

(saying that, he looks at the clock which is showing 9:10)

My God! What does this mean, this clock is showing 9:10! Why is it much later than that! The clock must be stopped—Griffo do you know why this clock is stopped at the same time exactly as my watch—this clock—

SAVILIA

(returning)

Yes, you are right—it's a strange thing and I noticed myself; this clock stopped this morning without any reason.

FABIEN

(very emotional)

This morning! Why—no question someone forgot to rewind it, mother?

SAVILIA

No, and that's what I don't understand, it is rewound the day before yesterday.

FABIEN

Oh, my God! My God!

SAVILIA

What's the matter with you, child?

FABIEN

Nothing, mother, nothing. Good night, mother.

SAVILIA

Goodnight, Fabien.

(near the door at the left, aside)

There is something unknown and terrible soaring around us.

(she leaves)

FABIEN

To horse, to horse, Griffo! Not a moment! As for me, I'm writing at all cost to my brother, you will deliver the letter to the post, so that it can leave by steamboat tomorrow; go, in five minutes return to receive it.

(Exit Griffo.)

FABIEN

This pain in my breast, this coincidence between my watch and the clock.

(throwing off his coat)

Nothing, nothing, yet—

(he remains in his shirtsleeves and sits at the table on the right and begins writing)

"My brother, my dear Louis, if this letter finds you still living, write me immediately two words to reassure me. I have had a terrible warning; write me, write me."

(he folds his letter and seals it; at the same time, Louis dei Franchi appears dressed as his brother, but with a bloodstain on his breast)

LOUIS

(uttering a sigh)

Ah!

FABIEN

(turning)

My brother—dead!

SAVILIA

(appearing in the doorway on the left)

Who said "dead"?

LOUIS

(finger on his mouth and to Fabien)

Silence! Look!

(He walks backwards and passes through the wall and disappears. At the same moment, the room in the back rises and a clearing in the Forest of Fontainbleau. On one side is a young man wiping off his sword—on the other Louis dei Franchi is lying between his two witnesses who are trying to help him.)

# CURTAIN

## ACT II
### SCENE 2

*The Opera—the gallery between the foyer and the ledges.*

*Masks, dominoes, cavaliers, in ball dress, strolling and meeting, talking, a bouquet seller offering her bouquets. Animated scene of the entrance to the foyer of the Opera on the night of a masked ball. After a moment, one sees Louis dei Franchi enter from the right. He comes forward, strolling, glancing at the crowd like a man seeing someone, during this scene, quadrilles can be heard playing in the background.*

LOUIS

(stopping and looking at his watch)

Soon it'll be 1:30. It's an hour that someone gave me a meeting—here—at the entrance to the foyer. I cannot doubt—this letter to Mr. Louis dei Franchi is indeed for me. Here it is twenty times that I've wandered through this gallery examining each domino that passes by, without knowing yet how to find the person

I am seeking—alas, perhaps it would be better if I do not find her—perhaps it would be better if I had not come but where should one go? One goes where destiny pushes you, and the proof is that I came, that I am waiting, that I am dying of impatience to meet this mysterious unknown! O Emilie! Emilie! To what tortures you condemn me. Let's see, search, search again.

MONTGIRON

(stopping, and to two or three young people who appear with him)

So, gentlemen, it's agreed, each to his own business, but at three o'clock, meet at my place for supper, right?

THE YOUNG PEOPLE

At three o'clock, yes, yes, it's agreed.

(They shake hands with Montgiron and Giordano and distance themselves.)

LOUIS

(returning to himself)

Useless to look, I don't see—

MONTGIRON

(who has left his friends, and taken Giordano's arm, crosses the stage and meets Louis)

Eh! Why, it's Louis dei Franchi.

GIORDANO

Louis!

LOUIS

Montgiron.

(very surprised)

And Giordano.

MONTGIRON

Eh! Yes, by Jove, the Baron Giordano Martelli, a compatriot of yours, I think.

LOUIS

Yes, yes—the two of us are from the Province of Sartene and friends from childhood.

GIORDANO

This good Louis. But let's hug each other.

(they hug)

And your brother, that fine Fabien?

LOUIS

I wrote to him, three weeks ago to recommend a friend who proposes to visit Corsica—ah, indeed, your regiment is no longer in Africa.

GIORDANO

Actually yes, but I'm on leave.

MONTGIRON

Could they refuse it to a hero of Mitidja?

LOUIS

Yes, I know you distinguished yourself down there, that you received the cross, and you were made Captain.

MONTGIRON

At twenty-three—that's me.

LOUIS

I learned all that from the Monitor and with great joy, I'll answer for that.

GIORDANO

Thanks, dear friend.

LOUIS

And how long have you been at Paris?

GIORDANO

Since this morning; I came here only for mid-Lent.

MONTGIRON

Also, you see, here he is at the opera, mixing myrtles with laurels.

GIORDANO

(to Louis)

And you, look, what are you doing? What's become of you since our separation?

LOUIS

(distracted)

Me?

MONTGIRON

He's in the process of getting himself received as a

lawyer.

GIORDANO

Lawyer!

MONTGIRON

(gaily)

Salute, Captain, *Cedant arma togae.*

(to Louis)

By the way, my dear friend, are you one of us?

LOUIS

One of you?

MONTGIRON

Yes, we are dining tonight at my place with some friends, Beauchamp, Favrolles, Château-Renaud.

LOUIS

(excitedly)

Château-Renaud?

MONTGIRON

You know him?

LOUIS

Only by sight, for having met him two or three times in society, that's all.

MONTGIRON

He's a lad very sought after, very refined, well versed in all arms, a man of fashion, a ladies' man—although between ourselves, I think he gets credit in that regard for more than he has, really.

LOUIS

(excitedly)

You believe that?

MONTGIRON

Yes, I think that he profits a lot on the reputation of a woman.

LOUIS

(aside)

If it's true, my God.

MONTGIRON

So indeed, it's decided you will come, won't you.

LOUIS

A thousand thanks, my dear Montgiron, but to my great regret, I cannot accept.

MONTGIRON

What! You cannot.

GIORDANO

And why's that—?

LOUIS

(embarrassed)

Why because I am waiting for someone here.

MONTGIRON

(gaily)

Well, it seems to me that it goes without saying that everybody has the right to bring his someone along. It is perfectly agreed that there will be five or six carafes of water with no other destiny than to hold fresh bouquets.

LOUIS

Yes, that's possible, but—

MONTGIRON

What now?

LOUIS

Heavens, it's necessary to tell you that I feel myself not in the mood to share in your pleasures.

GIORDANO

Indeed, what a concerned, preoccupied air—

MONTGIRON

Could you have some vexation?

GIORDANO

(with interest)

Some pain.

LOUIS

Yes, perhaps.

MONTGIRON

Why then, all the more reason to seek to distract yourself. It must be for this purpose that you came to the opera.

LOUIS

You are mistaken, for I came here probably to find anguishing news.

GIORDANO

Poor friend! I understand. It's a question of a flirt who is making game of your love.

LOUIS

No, but of a poor woman I want to save, who is ruining herself.

GIORDANO

And it's she you are awaiting?

LOUIS

Her, no—yesterday I received an anonymous letter in which they told me that if I was curious to have certain information about the person I am speaking to you about, a friend (the world swarms with friends like that) a friend would take the responsibility of communicating with me, and gave me a rendezvous here at one o'clock at the Opera in the gallery of the foyer.

MONTGIRON

At one o'clock! Why it's later than that—this lady won't come and in your place, my dear fellow , I would forget this adventure and come to dine.

GIORDANO

Montgiron's right, come with us.

LOUIS

No, gentlemen, no; thanks one more time for your persistence, but I have to stay here.

MONTGIRON

Come then, so be it, let's not speak of it any further.

GIORDANO

But at least, this person has indicated a sign by which you can recognize her?

MONTGIRON

Yes, she wrote me that I will recognize her by a bouquet of myositis that she will offer me by hand.

GIORDANO

A bouquet of myositis.

MONTGIRON

(noticing a domino who has entered carrying a bouquet of myositis)

Oh, indeed! Look there, my dear friend, that domino—isn't she the one you are waiting for?

LOUIS

(with emotion)

Indeed, those flowers.

MONTGIRON

She seems to be observing you—she's coming to you.

DOMINO

(who has come closer, bit by bit, touching his arm)

Louis dei Franchi.

LOUIS

(aside)

It's she!

(low to Domino)

You have to say something to me?

DOMINO

(low)

On behalf of Emilie—yes! But there are too many people here—offer me your arm and come—

LOUIS

(to Montgiron and Giordano)

I am leaving you, my friends.

GIORDANO

Why you aren't leaving the ball, we will see each other again?

LOUIS

Yes, tonight, perhaps or tomorrow.

(moving apart with the Domino—aside)

Oh, my God! My God! What am I going to learn?

GIORDANO

(watching him move away)

Poor lad, I fear he is embarking on some nasty business.

MONTGIRON

(laughing)

Right! The tortures of love—we've all been through that; in a few days he'll be consoled.

GIORDANO

That woman with whom he seems so occupied—do you know who she is?

MONTGIRON

No, truly! Of the devil himself, if I suspected he was amorous. He's an impenetrable young man, is our friend dei Franchi—he doesn't resemble that indiscreet of a Château-Renaud.

CHÂTEAU-RENAUD

(who's just entered)

Huh? What's that about?

MONTGIRON

Heavens, it's you, my dear chap—you were there.

CHÂTEAU-RENAUD

Yes, I was passing by! Evening, Montgiron.

MONTGIRON

Good evening, amusing yourself here?

CHÂTEAU-RENAUD

Fie! What do you take me for? Can we be amused at an Opera Ball? This is a pretext for supper; that's all. But, pardon, you were talking with this gentleman; I am disturbing you.

(he starts to move away)

MONTGIRON

In no way! And hold on, I was just speaking of you.

CHÂTEAU-RENAUD

I'm well aware.

MONTGIRON

Ah! Bah!

CHÂTEAU-RENAUD

That's why I'm one too many.

MONTGIRON

Why no, stay!

(Giordano, presenting Château-Renaud)

Mr. de Château-Renaud.

(to Château-Renaud)

The Baron Giordano Martelli, Captain in the First Regiment of African Cavalry.

(the two young men bow to each other)

CHÂTEAU-RENAUD

Well! Look here, gentlemen, what were you saying about me?

MONTGIRON

(laughing)

Why nothing bad, by Jove!

CHÂTEAU-RENAUD

That's the way I took it, but still—?

MONTGIRON

Well, I was repeating to Giordano what I had just been

saying to another of my friends, Louis dei Franchi.

CHÂTEAU-RENAUD

Louis dei Franchi! Ah, that gentleman is here—!

MONTGIRON

I was saying that you were accustomed to boast a little freely of your conquests—of those you made and even of those you had not made.

CHÂTEAU-RENAUD

Ha! Ha! And on the subject of my real conquests or imagined, were you pretending—very expensive?

MONTGIRON

Why on the subject of all of them in general.

CHÂTEAU-RENAUD

The Devil! You know the proverb: He who tries to prove too much proves nothing! Cite an example in support!

MONTGIRON

An example!

CHÂTEAU-RENAUD

Yes, a single one!

MONTGIRON

Madame de Lesparre.

CHÂTEAU-RENAUD

Emilie de Lesparre?

MONTGIRON

(ironic)

Yes, they pretend, they even affirm, my dear chap, that for the two months you paid assiduous court to her, you obtained far less from her than you seek to make it believed.

CHÂTEAU-RENAUD

Ah! They pretend that? And who might that be?

MONTGIRON

Why almost everybody.

CHÂTEAU-RENAUD

And you?

MONTGIRON

Oh! As for me, I'm accustomed to be of the opinion of the majority.

CHÂTEAU-RENAUD

Then you think I am a fop?

MONTGIRON

Damn!

CHÂTEAU-RENAUD

That I'm a boaster?

MONTGIRON

My word!

GIORDANO

(interposing)

Gentlemen!

CHÂTEAU-RENAUD

Don't worry—it's only a question of a simple wager!

(Montgiron)

Look—would you bet?

MONTGIRON

What?

CHÂTEAU-RENAUD

So I can give you proof—

MONTGIRON

Proof—of what sort?

CHÂTEAU-RENAUD

Whatever you like; for example, if I were tonight at the ball, make you see that lady on my arm?

MONTGIRON

Ah! Bah! Is she at the Opera?

CHÂTEAU-RENAUD

(negligently)

Yes, I think so, in a booth. Moreover, whether she is or isn't—do you agree to my proposition?

MONTGIRON

Eh! No! That wouldn't be a proof. All women can come

to a ball at the Opera, stroll about on the arm of a cavalier that they know without the least significance.

CHÂTEAU-RENAUD

Well! If I were to bring her to supper with you tonight?

MONTGIRON

Oh! That—that's another matter. But I defy you to do it!

CHÂTEAU-RENAUD

You defy me to do it?

MONTGIRON

Yes!

CHÂTEAU-RENAUD

What shall we bet?

MONTGIRON

You decide.

CHÂTEAU-RENAUD

A supper within three days for all our guests.

MONTGIRON

So be it!

CHÂTEAU-RENAUD

And how long will you give me to win the bet?

MONTGIRON

Until four o'clock, at four o'clock precisely, if you are not at my place with Madame de Lesparre, you will have lost.

CHÂTEAU-RENAUD

It's agreed! Until later, Montgiron.

MONTGIRON

Until later!

(he leaves with Giordano)

CHÂTEAU-RENAUD

Ah! Beautiful Emilie, for the two months you encouraged my love you let me conceive the most charming hopes—you were beginning the most delicious novel with me. Then, one day, by a whim, I don't know by what absurd scruple, it pleased you to close the book, and you thought everything had been said.

Come now, I would also be very naive! As for Mr. Château-Renaud, tricked, made a fool of, by a woman just a debutante, a school girl—! No, my darling! I am obstinate; if you have your reputation to defend, well, I have mine to preserve, and I will know how to compromise you to the degree so that necessarily you will end by being mine! But hush! The box is opening, it's she!

(Emilie emerging from the lodge facing him, very upset.)

EMILIE

(aside)

He's alone, come!

CHÂTEAU-RENAUD

At last you're here, Madame.

EMILIE

You demanded that I come and I came—at the risk of compromising myself—of ruining myself.

CHÂTEAU-RENAUD

What have you to fear—? Under this domino, this mask, who could recognize you?

EMILIE

Eh! My God! Do I know? Hasn't slander already attached itself to me? And if some of your friends or mine were to see me with you! Finally, I've fulfilled the condition that you imposed on me, in your turn you will keep your promise—those letters, you've brought them, haven't you?

CHÂTEAU-RENAUD

Yes, they are here.

EMILIE

And you are going to deliver them to me?

CHÂTEAU-RENAUD

No question—since you demand it! But one moment more, do me the favor of accepting my arm!

EMILIE

Remain in the midst of this crowd! Ah! Be generous, return those letter to me; leave me, leave.

CHÂTEAU-RENAUD

Leave, already! When this meeting is perhaps the last. No, no, that's impossible, you won't leave me like that, before having heard me, before having told me—

EMILIE

Eh! What more do you want me to tell you?

CHÂTEAU-RENAUD

Apprise me at least, the cause of this abrupt change, of this rupture that desolates me—why having received me, greeted me at first? Why did you give me these hopes? Why these charming letters that I considered as so many proofs of a shared love, and that you are today so coldly demanding back?

EMILIE

Yes, I feel that I must appear to you capricious, coquettish—and yet, I am not wicked. United by my father to a man, I hardly know then separated from him with having had the time to love him—delivered alone—without defense to the dangers of society, my heart allowed itself to be led to seduction, I slid to the edge of the abyss, and I was going to fall, perhaps, when I received a warning from a friend.

CHÂTEAU-RENAUD

From a friend?

EMILIE

Yes, a letter that opened my eyes, which recalled me to my duties, I had been imprudent, I didn't want to become sinful! What seems to you coquettish was only righteousness. What you call caprice, I call remorse.

CHÂTEAU-RENAUD

(with scorn)

And this officious friend—so devoted the author of this salutary message is no question Mr. Louis dei Franchi?

EMILIE

Him or someone else, what's it matter?

CHÂTEAU-RENAUD

Mr. Louis, who, if I am correctly informed, knew you before your marriage, Mr. Louis, who since his arrival in Paris, has seen you again frequently, who perhaps, nourishes secret hopes!

EMILIE

Him!

CHÂTEAU-RENAUD

Isn't he a lawyer? And it isn't the custom of his colleagues to give free consultations.

EMILIE

(offended)

Sir!

CHÂTEAU-RENAUD

(aside)

And I was hesitating when my vanity was involved—where I risk by withdrawing to make room for a rival!

EMILIE

(with a look at the back)

My God! The crowd is coming this way—those letter—I beg you—those letters?

CHÂTEAU-RENAUD

Those letters, well yes, I will keep my word, I will return to you, much later, this morning and on one condition.

EMILIE

Ah! You are an egoist—and cruel, sir.

CHÂTEAU-RENAUD

Egoist, yes—if it's to be an egoist to delay the moment of our separation. Cruel, no, because what I am asking of you.

EMILIE

Well—?

CHÂTEAU-RENAUD

(looking)

I notice some friends—! Distance yourself—in a moment, I will rejoin you and you will know—

(Emilie escapes. Montgiron has just reentered with Giordano by the left. Looks at her moving away and smiles.)

MONTGIRON

(laughing)

Ah! Ah! It seems that my arrival makes the pigeons fly off!

(going to Château-Renaud)

Well, my dear chap, you've seen Madame de Lesparre?

CHÂTEAU-RENAUD

Perhaps, indeed.

MONTGIRON

And the bet is still on?

CHÂTEAU-RENAUD

More than ever!

LOUIS

(aside)

A bet—what about?

CHÂTEAU-RENAUD

I'll even double it if you like.

MONTGIRON

Oh! Oh! What self confidence! So then, tonight.

CHÂTEAU-RENAUD

Tonight, my dear fellow. Madame de Lesparre will sup with us at your place.

LOUIS

(aside)

Great God!

(Château-Renaud leaves excitedly. Louis collapses on one of the benches at the bach)

GIORDANO

(noticing Louis, and going to him)

Louis! Well—that domino—she told you—?

LOUIS

Yes, I know now all that I wanted to know.

(to Montgiron)

My dear Montgiron, you were gracious enough to invite me to dine with you.

MONTGIRON

Yes, and you refused me.

LOUIS

That's true, but I've changed my mind since—

MONTGIRON

Bah! And now!

LOUIS

Now I accept.

MONTGIRON

Bravo!

GIORDANO

(watching Louis, aside)

This is strange.

MONTGIRON

At three, then, gentlemen.

THE OTHER TWO

At three o'clock.

(They move to different sides. Giordano follows Louis. The crowd has disappeared.)

**CURTAIN**

# ACT II
## SCENE 3

*Montgiron's home.*

*A bachelor salon very elegantly furnished. Entrance door at the back. Through a small door at the left can be seen a larger room with a table richly set. To the right, a chimney with a clock.*

**SERVANT**

(entering from the back and introducing the two young men)

Please take the trouble of coming in, gentlemen.

**LOUIS**

Mr. de Montgiron has not yet returned?

**SERVANT**

My Master, no, gentlemen, not yet.

GIORDANO

In that case, we'll wait for him.

SERVANT

You gentlemen are without doubt invited to dine?

GIORDANO

Yes.

SERVANT

Then that's wonderful; you won't have to wait long; the supper is for three o'clock, and that's only a few minutes from now.

GIORDANO

That's fine!

SERVANT

The gentlemen have need of me?

GIORDANO

You can leave us.

SERVANT

Suffice, gentlemen.

(he leaves)

(Louis has taken a seat and seems absorbed in his reflections. Giordano watches him a few moments in silence then he approaches him and takes his hand.)

GIORDANO

Louis, you are unhappy—you are ill!

LOUIS

Me?

GIORDANO

Yourself—! While we were in the crowd, where other ears than mine could hear you, I didn't ask any questions, I respected your silence—but here we are alone, and you can confide your secret to me. You know that pain confided to a friend lightens it by half, look, you don't doubt my discretion, my heart?

LOUIS

(offering him his hand)

No, Giordano, no.

GIORDANO

Well, then, tell me, what's bothering you, what's

affecting you! It's a question of love, isn't it?

LOUIS

Yes, of a love that blossomed under our beautiful Corsican sky—ravishing vision vanishing in our orange tree forest—the sweet and first song of a heart of twenty that the breeze brought me and that the storm took from me.

GIORDANO

Come on, talk—tell me everything.

(sitting near Louis)

LOUIS

Then listen, friend. This woman, I told you, I had loved back there, at her departure from Ajaccio, knowing that she was going to Paris, I decided to follow her; I left everything, my country, my mother, my excellent brother, so good, so generous—because he loved her, too—

GIORDANO

He loved her!

LOUIS

Who didn't love her? At last, after two months, I

arrived in Paris, full of hope, quite emotional over the thought that I am going to find myself near her—judge my pain when, on arriving, I found she was married.

GIORDANO

Married!

LOUIS

Yes, married without love, married when I came to request her hand.

GIORDANO

Ah! I understand your regrets, your sorrow! Still, you've seen this woman again?

LOUIS

To my misfortune, perhaps, yes, some time later, chance made me meet her. I had been received at the home of her father, during her visit to Corsica so I was not a stranger to her. She engaged me to go see her. I ought to have avoided her, fled her; I didn't have the courage. I went to her place; there, she presented me to her husband, and old friend of her father, a captain of the frigate, honest, frank, believing all men incapable of baseness because he himself had never committed any. His greeting touched me. I decided to be worthy of his confidence. I continued to frequent his house, well determined to combat, to kill my passion. I thought a holy friendship could succeed love. Soon I noticed the contrary, and too honest to abuse the hospitality that was offered to me, I ended my visits completely.

(he rises)

GIORDANO

Fine, very fine, friend.

LOUIS

Some time after that, I received a visit from the husband; he came to complain of my forgetfulness, of my indifference, than I told him frankly the truth—that is to say that his wife was too seductive for me to expose myself to the frequent sight of her—he smiled and offered me his hand—"My dear, Louis," he said to me, "in a few days I am leaving for Mexico, perhaps I will remain absent six months, perhaps a year—we sailors, we know the hour of departure, but never that of return—

My wife is young, beautiful, she's going to find herself deprived of her support, of her natural defender; I commend her to you in my absence; be her friend, her guardian angel, her brother."

GIORDANO

It is possible?

LOUIS

I remained stupefied and in my confusion, I promised—a week later, the captain departed. From that moment, began for me the perilous role he'd entrusted me with—but the thought that I could be useful to the one I loved, this protection that in default of love I was extending over her, the idea that if I could not adore my idol, I would not least preserve her purity, all this gave me strength, courage—I had no need to tell her that while loving her more than a brother ought, I no longer looked at her except as a sister.

GIORDANO

What then? What next?

LOUIS

(sitting back down)

She lived very retired; besides myself and a few intimate friends, no one frequented her house, until the day Mr. Château-Renaud was presented to her.

GIORDANO

(excitedly)

Mr. Château-Renaud?

LOUIS

What's the matter with you?

GIORDANO

Nothing. Continue.

LOUIS

You believe in omens, don't you? At his appearance, I shivered. He didn't say a word to me; he was what a man of the world ought to be, and yet when he left, I already hated him.

GIORDANO

(rising)

Yes, yes, I suspected as much. I understood that there was between that man and you one of those mysterious relationships of which a woman is a lightening rod. The one you love is named Madame de Lesparre?

LOUIS

What! You know? Well, yes, it's she! It's Emilie!

GIORDANO

(moving to the left)

In that case, I guess the rest, Mr. Château-Renaud pleased her; experienced in seductions, he spared nothing to make himself loved by her—

LOUIS

(rising and going to Giordano)

Yes, and soon it seemed to me I was not the only one to notice the preference she accorded him. My decision was taken, I decided to speak to Emilie about it, convinced as I still was that as yet on her part there was nothing of consequence—but to my great astonishment, Emilie took my observations as a joke, pretending. I was crazy, and that those who shared my ideas were as crazy as me. From then on, you grasp, my role became ridiculous—almost odious; I stopped going to Emilie's—In studying, I sought to forget the ideas that were tearing me apart; vain hope! The rumors that had assailed me in society came to seek me even in my retreat. I wanted to make a supreme effort; I wrote to Emilie to remind her of her obligations, to avoid the gulf into which she was about to fall, conjuring her, if there was still time to stop on this funeral slope. I received ny reply, I concluded from that that the evil was beyond remedy, and that Emilie was the mistress of Mr. Château-Renaud! What can I say to you? A deep pain seized me, pain that increased with the thought that suffering here I was making my poor brother suffer back there! Yes, sir, as result of the fatality that pursues me, I went to the Opera and there, after having learned from that unknown that had given me the rendezvous that Emilie was at the ball, I was witness to this outrageous bet which dishonors her.

(putting his hand to his eyes)

GIORDANO

(after a moment of silence)

My friend, would you permit me to give you some advice?

LOUIS

Speak!

GIORDANO

Trust me, don't be present at this supper.

LOUIS

What! I should leave?

GIORDANO

Heavens, yes, that would be better.

LOUIS

It's possible and indeed I feel you are right, but can

one always do what one ought to do? I admit I ought to scorn this woman, I admit that I am wrong to remain—and still, I am remaining.

GIORDANO

You are staying?

LOUIS

Yes, it's decided! If she comes, I intend to be there to confound her, to force her to blush, that will be her punishment; that will be my vengeance.

GIORDANO

(going to him)

Well, so be it! But at least be calm, courageous. It is evident that if she comes to dine with this man she doesn't know, with people she doesn't know anymore, she's a coquette. A coquette is not worthy of the love of a gallant man.

LOUIS

It's true, it's true—and yet.

(Noisy laughing outside.)

GIORDANO

Silence! They're coming.

MONTGIRON

This way, this way, ladies and gentlemen.

ESTHER

Ah! We've arrived! This is your place, Montgiron?

(looking around her)

Not bad for a bachelor's apartment.

GRAIN D'OR

Good grief! What luxury! Flowers on étagères—silk on the armchairs—and silk on the servants!

ESTHER

Ah, indeed! There's no one to fascinate here—can one remove one's mask?

MONTGIRON

By Jove!

ESTHER

In that case, ladies—down with wolves!

ALL

Down with the masks.

(They take off their masks, go to place their bouquets, and arrange their dress; meanwhile, Montgiron is approached by Louis and Giordano.)

MONTGIRON

Ah! You were there, gentlemen? Pardon for being made to wait by me; but you know one has always a quarter of an hour's grace.

GIORDANO

What of it, my dear friend, that's very fair.

MONTGIRON

(presenting the young men)

Mr. Beauchamp, Mr. Favrolles.

(they bow)

As for these ladies—

ESTHER

(coming up)

Bah! It's not worth the bother of presenting us; we are known.

MONTGIRON

(laughing)

Very advantageously, my pretty.

GRAIN D'OR

They're flattering!

LOUIS

(aside)

And it's among these women he dares to bring—

ESTHER

Well! Say, since all the presentations are made, if we can eat, I'm so starved.

ALL

And me, too.

MONTGIRON

Pardon, dear Esther; but I beg you, as well as my other guests, to be a bit patient.

GRAIN D'OR

I'd prefer to have a bit of stew.

ESTHER

Havens! And why should we? Wasn't it at three o'clock, we were supposed to have supper? Or indeed the champagne is not ready.

MONTGIRON

Yes, truly; but a slight variation has occurred unexpectedly.

ESTHER

Not to supper, at least?

MONTGIRON

No, no—rest assured, only I will ask you to wait till four o'clock.

ESTHER AND THE OTHER WOMEN

Ah! Good God!

MONTGIRON

And to make the most furious appetites doze off, as I came in, I gave François the order to bring us Madeira.

ESTHER

Go for the Madeira! I will soak a biscuit.

(François enters with a platter that he places on a small round table.)

MONTGIRON

Come, ladies, come gentlemen.

(Everybody surrounds the table except Louis, who remains in the foreground.)

GRAIN D'OR

(after having had a drink)

Ah, indeed! You are still waiting for someone?

MONTGIRON

Yes.

ESTHER

And who is this someone who is late?

MONTGIRON

Château-Renaud.

ALL THE WOMEN

Château-Renaud.

MONTGIRON

I promised to give him until four o'clock, as it is a question of a bet.

SOMEONE

Of a bet?

MONTGIRON

Yes, I bet him a supper for a dozen guests, that he won't bring us a certain lady that he engaged himself to bring to us.

LOUIS

(aside)

How I suffer!

ESTHER

And who is this beauty of such proud virtue that one

makes such bets about her?

(Louis became attentive)

POMPONETTE

Must be a prude—a Joan of Arc?

MONTGIRON

My work, I think it's no great indiscretion to name the mask—it's Madame—

LOUIS

(rising and placing his hand on the arm of Montgiron)

Montgiron in favor of our friendship, grant me a favor.

MONTGIRON

A favor, my friend, what is it?

LOUIS

Don't name the person who has to come with Mr. Château-Renaud.

MONTGIRON

And why?

LOUIS

You know she's a married woman.

POMPONETTE

(laughing)

A married woman! Heavens, that's even funnier!

MONTGIRON

Yes, but whose husband is in Smyrna, the Indies, Mexico, I don't know where?

GRAIN D'OR

The unfortunate.

(laughing)

I pity him.

(they laugh)

MONTGIRON

As for a husband so distant, you know, it's as if one didn't have one—

ESTHER

That counts only in the Bureau of Vital Statistics—

under birth certificates.

ALL

(laughing)

Ha, ha, ha—

LOUIS

(gravely)

Her husband will return in a few days; I know him, he's a man of honor, worthy of all respect—and I would like, if possible, to spare him the chagrin of learning on his return that his wife, if she comes, has committed such a fault.

MONTGIRON

Ah, my dear friend, excuse me. I was unaware that you knew this lady, I doubted even that she was married, but since you know her, since you know the husband—

LOUIS

I know them.

MONTGIRON

We will place it all under the greatest discretion.

(to his guests)

Gentlemen and ladies, whether Château-Renaud comes or doesn't come, whether he comes alone or he comes accompanied, whether he wins or loses his bet. I demand that you keep this adventure secret.

ALL

Why of course! We promise you!

ESTHER

I swear it.

LOUIS

(opening his hand to Montgiron)

Thanks, Montgiron, thanks! I assure you that you've just performed the act of a gallant man.

GRAIN D'OR

So, you say that Mr. Château-Renaud has until four o'clock? I advise him to hurry for it is ten minutes till.

LOUIS

(to Montgiron, looking at the clock)

Is your clock right?

MONTGIRON

Ah, my word, that's not my worry that concerns Château-Renaud, I sent to set my clock by his watch so he cannot complain of having been surprised.

ESTHER

Ah! Bah! gentlemen, since we cannot speak openly of Château-Renaud and his unknown let's not speak of him at all, for we will fall into enigmas, charades, riddles—and that won't be amusing.

MONTGIRON

Esther's right, there are so many women who are not charades, of whom one can speak, and who ask nothing better than to be spoken of.

ESTHER

(raising her glass)

To the health of those women.

ALL (except Louis)

Yes! Yes! To their health.

GIORDANO

(low to Louis)

Why in that case drink—you see plainly he won't come.

LOUIS

(low, always looking at the clock)

He still has five minutes.

GIORDANO

(low)

Never mind—luck is with you.

LOUIS

(low and smiling)

At four o'clock, my friend, however late I may be I promise you to catch up with the others.

GIORDANO

(moving away a bit, aside)

Poor Louis—

LOUIS

(eyes fixed on the clock, aside as others drink around the table)

How slowly the hand advances! One might say, to see it pursue its impassive progress, that on it are suspended my hope and life! My God! But the hour I am waiting for—won't it ever strike?

(moment of silence)

(the first bell of four o'clock)

Ah!

ALL

Ah!

GIORDANO

(excitedly to Louis)

To your health!

(Louis takes a glass and places it to his lips as the hour continues to ring. At the 4th blow the noise of ringing in the antechamber.)

LOUIS

(putting down his glass and shivering)

That's him.

GIORDANO

Yes, but perhaps it's not her.

MONTGIRON

(rushing to the door at the back)

That we are going to see momentarily.

(he vanishes for a moment; everyone turns toward the back with curiosity)

LOUIS

(grasping Giordano's arm)

My friend, it seems to me I recognized her voice.

GIORDANO

(low)

Think what you promised me: to be calm and courageous.

MONTGIRON

(outside)

But I beg you, Madame, come in, will you; I assure you, we are all friends here.

CHÂTEAU-RENAUD

(outside)

Eh, yes, come on then, my dear Emilie, you won't unmask, if you like.

LOUIS

(aside)

Wretch!

EMILIE

(dragged in by Montgiron)

Sir—sir—mercy.

CHÂTEAU-RENAUD

(appearing at the back)

Four o'clock rang as I arrived, gentlemen.

MONTGIRON

Very well, my dear fellow, you won.

EMILIE

(standing up with all her haughtiness)

Not yet, sir, for I understand your insistence now—you made a bet to bring me to supper here, right?

CHÂTEAU-RENAUD

Why—

EMILIE

Since that man won't reply, you reply, sir—Didn't Mr. Château-Renaud bet that he would bring me to supper with you—

MONTGIRON

I cannot hide from you, Madame, that Mr. Château-Renaud flattered me with that hope.

EMILIE

Well, Mr. Château-Renaud lost.

ALL

What's she say?

EMILIE

Yes, lost, for I was unaware where I was going, because to get me here, he employed a trick, a lie—he made me think he was taking me to one of my friends.

ALL

Is it possible?

EMILIE

(removing her mask)

Oh! I can unmask now, I no longer fear speaking to you with an uncovered face; for if someone here must blush, it seems to me, it's not me.

CHÂTEAU-RENAUD

Madame!

EMILIE

(calmly)

So, I was saying that since I didn't come voluntarily, Mr. Château-Renaud ought, in my opinion, to lose the benefits of the wager.

CHÂTEAU-RENAUD

Why, at least now that you are here, dear Madame, you will stay, won't you? See, we have good company in men and happy company in women—

EMILIE

Now that I am here, I shall again thank the gentleman who appears to me to be the master of the house, for the nice greeting that he wanted to give me, but as I cannot respond to his gracious invitation, I will beg Mr. Louis dei Franchi, my friend, to give me his arm and to escort me home.

LOUIS

(rushing to her)

Oh! I'm here at your orders, Madame.

ESTHER

(low to Château-Renaud)

You are robbed, my dear—

CHÂTEAU-RENAUD

(with concentrated hate)

Pardon, but I will observe to you, Madame, that it was I who brought you here, and that consequently, it's up to me to escort you back.

EMILIE

Gentlemen, you are five men here, I place myself under

the safeguard of your honor, you will, I trust, prevent Mr. Château-Renaud from doing me violence.

(Louis placed himself between her and Château-Renaud.)

CHÂTEAU-RENAUD

(after having repressed a gesture of scorn, very calmly)

That's fine, Madame,m you are free, I know to whom I must thank for this.

LOUIS

(coldly)

If it's to me, sir, you will find me at home all day.

CHÂTEAU-RENAUD

Suffice, sir, perhaps I won't have the honor of presenting myself in person, but in my place, you will indeed, I hope, receive two of my friends.

EMILIE

A duel!

ALL

Gentlemen!

LOUIS

(disdainfully)

All you lack is to give such a rendezvous before a woman.

(taking Emilie's arm)

Come, Madame, and believe that all my blood cannot pay for the honor you are doing me and the happiness I feel.

(he moves away by the back with Emilie)

GIORDANO

(aside)

A duel! Ah! That's what I was afraid of.

CHÂTEAU-RENAUD

(with forced gaiety)

Well, what gentlemen? I lost that's all. Day after tomorrow, all of you who are here—at the Provencal Brothers.

SERVANT

(entering)

The gentlemen are served.

CHÂTEAU-RENAUD

Let's eat then.

ALL

Let's eat.

GIORDANO

(going to his hat)

Oh! As for me, I'm not staying here!

(While everyone turns towards the room to the left where supper is waiting, Giordano leaves by the back.)

# CURTAIN

## ACT II
### SCENE 4

*A clearing in the Forest at Fontainbleau. Louis dei Franchi is on the ground, wounded, surrounded by his witnesses, Montgiron and Giordano. A surgeon is near him examining the wound. On the other side of the stage is Château-Renaud wiping his sword; two other witnesses are near him. It's the exact reproduction of the scene that terminated the first act.*

GIORDANO

(to surgeon)

Well, doctor.

SURGEON

The sword went through through the lung—the condition of the wound leaves me no hope.

MONTGIRON

(overwhelmed)

My God! What a misfortune!

GIORDANO

(looking at his watch, aside)

Ten past nine; poor friend! He really told me.

LOUIS

(coming to and rising)

Montgiron—Giordano—where are you?

GIORDANO

Hear, near you!

MONTGIRON

(bending over him)

My friend, don't you have some wish, some will to express? Don't you want to charge me with the case of informing your family?

LOUIS

It's unnecessary; they will know.

MONTGIRON

When?

LOUIS

This evening.

MONTGIRON

And who will apprise them?

LOUIS

I will!

(he falls back into a faint)

(General astonishment. During these last words, the back of the stage opens slowly. The room in the first act is visible. The clock strikes 9:10—Madame dei Franchi is in the doorway and Fabien looking in the exact position they occupied.)

FABIEN

(to his mother who he places on her knees)

Pray for Louis, Mother, as for me, I am going to avenge him.

**CURTAIN**

# ACT III
## SCENE 5

*The clearing in the first of Fontainbleau where Louis was killed.*

**WOODCUTTER**

(cutting wood and singing)

It is a shepherdess
Lou, lou, la
It is a shepherdess
Who sings high, who sings low

(repeat)

In complaining of her misery
Lou, lou, la
In complaining of her misery.
The son of the King heard her.

(The distant noise of a post-chaise can be heard on the highway and the bells of horses, the woodcutter interrupts his work and goes to look through the trees.)

## WOODCUTTER

Clip, clop! And get going then! Now there's one making the dust. Are they going in a group! Oh! These rich folk, it is lucky to roll like that. Well! But what's the postilion doing? He's leading them right onto a bunch of rocks. Ah, indeed! He drank a cup too many this morning, that joker!

(shouting)

Hey, will you be careful imbecile—!

Why can't you see clearly?

Why you want to take a spill?

(uproar heard in the carriage which turns over)

Phooey! Now what was I saying? Goodnight, everybody! Everyone is on the ground—! That's well done! Why are those aristos going in a carriage!

(looking in the distance while padding down his pipe)

Heavens! It's two gentlemen who were in the carriage—there they are who can help themselves—they're looking to the right and left. They are looking for someone who can help them right their carriage—not often that I am going to trouble myself for folks who ride poste. Great! I think they have seen me—they have seen me all the same. My word, yes! They are making signs to me—yes, yes, call—go ahead.

(he sets back to work singing)

The son of the King heard her (repeat)
Who's that shepherdess—
Lou, Lou, la—
Who is that shepherdess—

CHÂTEAU-RENAUD

(enters from the back)

Hey, say, my honest fellow.

WOODCUTTER

(aside, and without troubling himself)

Right! There they are! The rick folks have from time to time need of their fellow creatures.

(sings)

Who is that Shepherdess?
Lou, Lou, la
Who is that Shepherdess?

CHÂTEAU-RENAUD

(striking him on the shoulder)

Well, friend, don't you hear, or rather don't you want to hear?

WOODCUTTER

(half turning)

It is to me you are speaking, sir?

CHÂTEAU-RENAUD

Why without doubt—and who else would it be?

WOODCUTTER

Ah, pardon, excuse, it's that I'm busy.

(rapping and humming)

The son of the King asked her (repeat)
Watcha doing there, Shepherdess?

CHÂTEAU-RENAUD

Come on, listen to me.

MONTGIRON

(approaching)

Besides, if we are disturbing you, my friend, it won't be for nothing, and we will indemnify you for your bother.

WOODCUTTER

(taking his pipe from his pocket and bowing)

Oh! In that case, it's different. What can I do to serve you, boss?

MONTGIRON

The axle of our carriage just broke.

WOODCUTTER

Ah, I know that perfectly well—I saw you turn over.

Ah—indeed, he took a vow to give you a spill; Papa Antoine?

MONTGIRON

(dusting himself off with his handkerchief)

Who is that, Papa Antoine?

WOODCUTTER

He's your postilion, well, look, what is it you want?

MONTGIRON

Do you know a wheelwright in Fontainbleau?

**WOODCUTTER**

I should say so—and a famous one at that! He's my cousin. Oh! He was born to be a carriage builder in Paris. But there no justice in the world.

**MONTGIRON**

Very fine—would you take it upon yourself to go find him—him and his tools.

**MONTGIRON**

You will have 10 francs, go!

**WOODCUTTER**

(excited)

Ten francs; I'm running.

**MONTGIRON**

Hurry—we are in a rush!

**WOODCUTTER**

In a short while, I will bring him to you.

(starts to leave, returns)

By the way, bosses, you didn't dislocate anything

where you fell.

MONTGIRON

No, thanks.

WOODCUTTER

Ah, see, my cousin is also a bit of a surgeon, veterinarian, bone-setter—and, while at the same time fixing your axle, he could also fix an arm or a leg.

MONTGIRON

We didn't break anything—luckily.

WOODCUTTER

So much the better! I'm going.

(starts to leave again, stop)

MONTGIRON

Go, and be quick about it.

(seeing him return)

Well—what is it, now?

WOODCUTTER

Say—ordinarily, a turnover makes you thirsty, you

wouldn't like to have something? You don't need refreshments?

MONTGIRON

(losing his patience)

No, indeed, animal, will you go!

WOODCUTTER

Ah, because my cousin is also a seller of spirits.

MONTGIRON

(pushing him by the shoulders)

Look, will you go?

WOODCUTTER

(leaving)

Don't be so impatient. I'll be back.

(he goes out by the left)

MONTGIRON

That's really fortunate.

(Montgiron goes to Château-Renaud, who has seated himself on a stone and has been holding his head in his hands)

Well, what's wrong now, Château-Renaud?

CHÂTEAU-RENAUD

Word of honor, my dear Montgiron, if I were superstitious, I'd have thought twice before setting out—that's what it is.

MONTGIRON

Indeed, I admit that this is a trip that has started badly.

CHÂTEAU-RENAUD

(rising)

Heavens, my dear fellow, I think we would have done as well to remain in Paris.

MONTGIRON

Oh, as for remaining in Paris, that's another matter. I've already given you my profession of faith as to that. Stay, if you wish, as for me, I'm leaving. The news of your duel with Louis, despite all the care we took to stifle the affair, is spread about and we have had the honor of being the subject of a very particular discussion between the King's attorney and the Minister of Justice.

CHÂTEAU-RENAUD

(pacing about uneasily)

Yes, I know, you already told me that, but what does it matter!

MONTGIRON

Oh! It's no joking matter dealing with gentlemen of the bar; for some while they have been looking for an opportunity to make an example. And as, unfortunately, this was not your first encounter, they would be enchanted to begin with you.

CHÂTEAU-RENAUD

Eh, my God! For two or three unfortunate affairs that one has had.

MONTGIRON

You wouldn't care more than I do to appear in Criminal Court? We'd be acquitted, it's true—but after spending three months in prison, which is not at all fun—without counting that you would be threatened with yet another difficulty.

CHÂTEAU-RENAUD

What's that?

MONTGIRON

You know that Louis dei Franchi had a brother.

CHÂTEAU-RENAUD

Yes—well—so what?

MONTGIRON

Well, that brother is a real Corsican, imbued with all the prejudices of his country. Who knows, after learning of the death of his brother, he won't drop everything, to come avenge him.

CHÂTEAU-RENAUD

Is that a reason? Because I fought with Mr. Louis dei Franchi that I am obliged to fight with all his family?

MONTGIRON

In France, no; in Corsica, yes—In the end, wait, Château-Renaud, I believe it is wiser to absent ourselves for several months; we will take a tour of Switzerland or the Midi of France; we will go wherever you like; but by our absence, we will be giving time for this deplorable affair to subside.

CHÂTEAU-RENAUD

Well, so be it, since you wish it, and because it's agreed

we won't change the plan in any way. Besides, me, too, I don't know what I have that urges me—to go where? To do what? I don't know anything about it; but something with fatality in it.

MONTGIRON

(laughing)

Ah! Ah! You, too, Château-Renaud! Château-Renaud! Fatalist!

CHÂTEAU-RENAUD

It's absurd, I know it; but what do you want; that's the way it is! I've seen the most solid minds, uneasy over a broken mirror or a howling dog. And I laughed at that superstition without suspecting that in my turn—

MONTGIRON

Well—in your turn?

CHÂTEAU-RENAUD

Look! It is an ordinary thing that this carriage overturns—and where? On the great highway.

MONTGIRON

It's an affair of a drunken postilion.

CHÂTEAU-RENAUD

My dear chap, the carriage didn't turn over because the postilion was drunk—no, the postilion was drunk because the carriage had to turn over.

MONTGIRON

Ah, indeed—why, you're going crazy.

CHÂTEAU-RENAUD

(pursuing his idea)

And that turned over—where? In the forest of Fontainbleau—in this forest where five days ago—

(looking around him with terror)

Eh! Wait! Wait!

MONTGIRON

What?

CHÂTEAU-RENAUD

Look! See!

MONTGIRON

What the devil's wrong with you?

CHÂTEAU-RENAUD

What! You don't recognize it—! You don't recognize the place when we are—? This clearing—this path! This tree?

MONTGIRON

(looking also)

Why, wait! Yes, indeed, it is the same place that five days ago almost the same time—

CHÂTEAU-RENAUD

What are you saying? Huh?

MONTGIRON

(more serious)

Indeed—it is strange!

CHÂTEAU-RENAUD

Ah—you admit it.

MONTGIRON

I admit the coincidence.

CHÂTEAU-RENAUD

Coincidence! Oh! There's more in this than coincidence, Montgiron—! There's fatality in it! Perhaps, the finger of God.

MONTGIRON

Calm down, I hear someone.

(going to the back)

It's our man.

WOODCUTTER

Oof! Here I am—I had a nice run—go!

MONTGIRON

Well—the carriage repairman?

WOODCUTTER

My cousin? He's already working on your carriage! Here, see him down there?

MONTGIRON

(looking)

That's fine! There's what I promised you.

(he gives him money)

WOODCUTTER

Thanks, boss.

MONTGIRON

Now, you can go back to work.

WOODCUTTER

To work! Ah, bah! Not often! Now that I've had a good day, I feel the need to give myself a little pleasure at the cabaret.

(hearing the noise of a post-chaise)

Great! There's a second carriage—now, if that one could turn over as well—

Your health, bosses, and bon voyage.

(he takes his hatchet and places his faggots on his shoulder)

What are you doing there, shepherdess?

(he leaves by the right)

CHÂTEAU-RENAUD

(agitated)

Let's go, my friend, let's go.

MONTGIRON

Where to?

CHÂTEAU-RENAUD

Wherever you like, my dear chap, but let's not stay here—! Do you see, I have need to walk about, to be out of this woods. The appearance of the clearing recalls memories to me that I would like to forget, it seems to me that everything is taking on a funereal appearance, a somber voice. It seems to me that from the midst of these trees that spectre of Louis dei Franchi is going to emerge—it seems to me.

MONTGIRON

Ah! What madness—

CHÂTEAU-RENAUD

I am crazy, it's possible, but it's like that! Let's go, Montgiron, let's go.

(staring to leave and noticing Fabien)

Ah!

FABIEN

(who has entered from the back)

Stay!

MONTGIRON

(aside, with emotion)

My God!

CHÂTEAU-RENAUD

(with terror, to Fabien)

What do you want?

FABIEN

Can't you guess, Mr. Château-Renaud?

CHÂTEAU-RENAUD

Louis dei Franchi.

FABIEN

No, not Louis; but Fabien, his brother.

CHÂTEAU-RENAUD

His brother!

MONTGIRON

(aside)

Ah! What I feared has happened.

FABIEN

(with a terrible calm, advancing or Château-Renaud who recoils)

Isn't it true, gentlemen, that the resemblance between the two of us was great? So great, that in seeing me appear you are asking yourselves if it isn't the spectre of Louis emerging from the tomb. No, gentlemen, no, I am not a spectre, I am a man, a man who five days ago was at the other end of Corsica, and who learned that he had lost his beloved brother, and who has come to demand of you, Mr. Château-Renaud: What have you done with my brother?

CHÂTEAU-RENAUD

(with a sort of arrogance)

Me? Me?

FABIEN

Yes, the reply of the first murderer, right? "You didn't give him to me to guard." Well, what you did, I am going to tell you. First of all you troubled his rest; you deflowered his life; you strove to stigmatize a woman on whom he placed his happiness in watching over; then one day through a lie, you caught this woman in a trap, after having hurled your defiance in the face of his defender, abusing against him your cleverness at swordsmanship—you murdered him!

(movement by the two men)

Murdered! I repeat the word. That's what you've done to my brother, sir.

MONTGIRON

(placing himself between them to Fabien)

Pardon, sir, but I don't understand; at the time of this fatal event, five days ago, you were in Corsica, you yourself just said so. How then were you able to come up with these sad details so rapidly?

FABIEN

You are forgetting the ballad, sir, the dead go fast.

MONTGIRON

Oh! Sir, you don't think us credulous enough, I suppose, to astound us, like children, with ghost stories?

FABIEN

(coldly)

The very evening of the death of Louis dei Franchi, I was fully instructed of everything. Of the quarrel, of the duel, of the name of the adversary. Not only was I instructed in all but I had seen everything, I left immediately, five days sufficed for me to do 280 leagues. Arrived just last night, this morning I presented myself at your home, you has just left in a post-chaise. In informed myself of the road you took and I followed you. From a distance, I saw a carriage overturned on the great highway and I said: God is stopping them.

CHÂTEAU-RENAUD

(resolutely)

In the end, sir, what do you want from me?

FABIEN

What do I want? A Corsican family is like an ancient hydra, no sooner has one head been beaten down than it pushes up another which gnaws and tears, in the place of one that is beaten down. What do I want, sir?

I want to kill the one who killed my brother.

CHÂTEAU-RENAUD

You want to kill me and how's that?

FABIEN

Oh! I don't worry! Not from behind a wall or through hay, in the fashion of my country, as they do things down there; no—as they do here—in the French manner—with white gloves, fulls and sleeves—and you see, sir, I am dressed for combat.

CHÂTEAU-RENAUD

Well, so be it, sir, my most ardent wish would have been to avoid this meeting and you see, I was fleeing it. But since you exact it, since you are coming to place yourself athwart my path, since you are running after misfortune, misfortune to you!

MONTGIRON

One moment, gentlemen, one moment, the custom in France, is not to make a duel a family heirloom. It's already quite enough of a misfortune that has taken place, and I oppose with all my power—

FABIEN

You didn't oppose the cause and you want to oppose

the effect! You haven't the right, Mr. Montgiron. Allow me to settle this business with Mr. Château-Renaud.

MONTGIRON

Say what you will, sir, but I won't suffer it.

FABIEN

Mr. Château-Renaud, against my sight, against my expectation, against the esteem of a swordsman that I hold him in default of other esteem, would Mr. Château-Renaud—refuse me the satisfaction I demand of him in the name of blood shed by him?

CHÂTEAU-RENAUD

I've not given anyone the right to suspect my courage, whoever it may be and from what source I fetch it—and you won't have that advantage over the others. So, I am placing myself entirely at your orders—but on one condition still—

FABIEN

I would have thought it was up to me to set conditions—never mind, speak!

CHÂTEAU-RENAUD

It's that this battle be the last, that after you, no other brother will come, no other cousin, that after you, I'll be left in peace.

FABIEN

This combat will be the last; I am Louis' only brother, and after me, after me, Mr. Château-Renaud, after me you will be at peace, it's I who say so.

CHÂTEAU-RENAUD

That suffices. Name yourself the hour, the weapons, the place.

FABIEN

The hour? I swore that it would be that in which I met you; the weapons—it is with the sword that you fought with my brother and the place? This place.

CHÂTEAU-RENAUD

This place?

FABIEN

Didn't you yourself choose it five days ago? Wasn't it here that you fought with my brother? Wasn't it at the foot of this tree that he fell? And if I searched carefully, if you dared to search with me, wouldn't we still find here traces of his blood?

CHÂTEAU-RENAUD

(resolutely)

Eh, well then, since you wish it, here, with swords, right now.

(removing his coat)

You are right, we must get it over with!

MONTGIRON

(going between them)

Gentlemen, gentlemen, this duel is impossible, for the moment at least; you don't have a single witness and no weapons.

FABIEN

You are mistaken, sir! We Corsicans, we are men of vengeance, as they call us, we do not allow ourselves to be taken unequipped this way and I've come with everything which is necessary for me.

(calling)

Come, Meynard.

(Alfred, entering from the back, swords in hand.)

FABIEN

Here's my witness—here are weapons.

MONTGIRON

(going to Alfred)

Ah, it's you, Meynard, so much the better! Tell me, is there no way—?

FABIEN

(who has removed his jacket)

Useless, Mr. Montgiron. Mr. Meynard knows what he has to do.

CHÂTEAU-RENAUD

Pardon! Sir, I'm waiting!

FABIEN

Meynard, beg Mr. Château-Renaud to choose the sword he likes.

ALFRED

(presenting swords to Château-Renaud)

Choose.

CHÂTEAU-RENAUD

(having taken a sword)

En garde, sir.

FABIEN

(coldly)

If you have some order to give, sir, give it.

CHÂTEAU-RENAUD

And why, sir?

FABIEN

Because, as sure as God is watching us, in 10 minutes you will be lying there in the place where my brother was lying.

CHÂTEAU-RENAUD

No bragging, sir.

FABIEN

(very calm)

I appeal to these gentlemen, do I seem a braggart?

(first combat lasting a few minutes in which Château-

Renaud uselessly wears himself out)

FABIEN

Let's rest a minute, sir, you are tired.

CHÂTEAU-RENAUD

(to Montgiron)

That man has got a steel wrist.

(after a moment)

Wherever you wish.

FABIEN

I still wish—

(the second battle, during which Château-Renaud sword is broken)

MONTGIRON

(rushing in)

Gentlemen, gentlemen, Mr. Château-Renaud's sword is broken; gentlemen, this combat cannot continue—the weapons are not equal.

FABIEN

Sir, you are mistaken.

(breaking his sword under his heel)

They are now.

(to Château-Renaud, presenting him with the broken sword)

Pick up that sword and let's continue.

MONTGIRON

Implacable.

FABIEN

As destiny!

(he has Alfred attach the sword to his wrist with his kerchief)

CHÂTEAU-RENAUD

(as he attaches his own sword to his wrist in the same manner, to Montgiron)

I am going to be killed, Montgiron! You will leave alone! In a week, you will write to my mother that I fell from my horse—in two weeks, you will write her that I am dead. If she were to learn this fatal news all at once, she would die of it herself.

MONTGIRON

You are mad, Château-Renaud.

CHÂTEAU-RENAUD

God is with that man, Montgiron.

ALFRED

Gentlemen.

(struggle, body to body. Château-Renaud knocks Fabien to the ground, but at the moment he raises his arm to strike him, Fabien plunges his weapon into his heart)

CHÂTEAU-RENAUD

(falling by the tree where Louis fell)

Ah! What did I tell you, Montgiron.

(he expires)

FABIEN

(distancing himself)

Mother. I kept my word. Louis! Louis! I can weep now.

(he breaks out in tears in Alfred's arms)

LOUIS

(appearing and resting his hand on Fabien's shoulder)

Hey, why weep for me, brother? Won't we see each other again, on high?

## CURTAIN

Note from the authors: The actor on tour, charged with the double role of Fabien and Louis must strive to give the role of Fabien a wild ferocity, and that of Louis a tincture of melancholy sweetness, a double physiognomy that Mr. Fechter knew how to imprint on these parts with so much talent and felicity.

# ABOUT THE AUTHOR

**Frank J. Morlock** has written and translated many plays since retiring from the legal profession in 1992. His translations have also appeared on Project Gutenberg, the Alexandre Dumas Père web page, Literature in the Age of Napoléon, Infinite Artistries.com, and Munsey's (formerly Blackmask). In 2006 he received an award from the North American Jules Verne Society for his translations of Verne's plays. He lives and works in México.

www.ingramcontent.com/pod-product-compliance
Lightning Source LLC
LaVergne TN
LVHW041623070426
835507LV00008B/413